D1433489

Columbia University

Contributions to Education

Teachers College Series

No. 756

AMS PRESS

NEW YORK

READING

AND

NINTH GRADE ACHIEVEMENT

BY EVA (BOND) WAGNER

SUBMITTED IN PARTIAL FULFILLMENT OF THE REQUIREMENTS
FOR THE DEGREE OF DOCTOR OF PHILOSOPHY IN THE
FACULTY OF PHILOSOPHY, COLUMBIA UNIVERSITY

Published with the Approval of
Professor Arthur I. Gates and Professor Helen M. Walker, Co-Sponsors

BUREAU OF PUBLICATIONS
TEACHERS COLLEGE, COLUMBIA UNIVERSITY
NEW YORK CITY
1938

Library of Congress Cataloging in Publication Data

Wagner, Eva (Bond) 1903-
    Reading and ninth grade achievement.

    Reprint of the 1938 ed., issued in series: Teachers
College, Columbia University. Contributions to educa-
tion, no. 756.
    Originally presented as the author's thesis, Columbia.
    Bibliography: p.
    1. Reading comprehension. 2. Mental tests.
3. Ninth grade (Education) 4. Achievement motivation.
I. Title. II. Series: Columbia University. Teachers
College. Contributions to education, no. 756.
LB1131.W327 1972   373.1'2'62   71-176792
ISBN 0-404-55756-2

Reprinted by Special Arrangement with Teachers
College Press, New York, New York

From the edition of 1938, New York
First AMS edition published in 1972
Manufactured in the United States

AMS PRESS, INC.
NEW YORK, N. Y.   10003

ACKNOWLEDGMENTS

I AM VERY HAPPY to be able to acknowledge in print my sincere appreciation of the kindness that was shown me at all times by many different people during the formulation and execution of this study. This is especially true with regard to Professor Arthur I. Gates, who has been an inspiration to me not only during my work on this book but also at every stage in my study of psychology.

I wish also to express my deep gratitude to Professor Helen M. Walker for her enthusiastic and untiring aid, which on several occasions proved to be the impetus that was needed to carry on with the statistical work involved.

In addition I wish to thank Professor Ruth Strang for reading the manuscript and Professor Irving Lorge for the statistical help he gave me during the formulation of the problem.

The teachers of the group of children with whom I worked were exceedingly cooperative, as were also Mr. W. L. Miller, City Superintendent of Schools, and Mr. Harry Dotson, Principal of the John Simpson Junior High School, Mansfield, Ohio. I wish to thank them for this cooperation.

EVA BOND

CONTENTS

CONTENTS

TABLES

FIGURES

ix

CHAPTER I

INTRODUCTION

STUDENTS IN HIGH SCHOOLS and colleges are displaying an increasing interest in the subject of reading. Wherever reading clinics have been established, a considerable proportion of the cases who seek help are high school and college students who feel, after conference with their advisers, that their own scholarship is impaired by reading disability.

The increasing interest in reading, which is manifested by educators, students, and laymen alike, was stated as one of the desirable trends in the field of reading by the Committee on Reading of the National Society for the Study of Education in its recent report.[1] Evidences of interest in reading may be found on every hand. Popular articles dealing with this subject [2] are appearing with great frequency in non-professional magazines. Reading clinics are being established not only by colleges and universities but also as community enterprises. The demand for extension courses in the teaching of reading is noticeably greater than it was several years ago. The courses offered by colleges of education in diagnosis of reading disabilities and the improvement of reading on both the elementary school level and the high school and college levels are well attended. That the volume of research in reading is very great is shown by the fact that the number of studies published since 1925 exceeds 1,200, which is more than twice the number reported during the preceding century.[3]

The following approaches to the subject of reading may be recognized in the literature:

Reading is regarded by some investigators as a relatively sim-

[1] *Thirty-Sixth Yearbook of the National Society for the Study of Education,* Part I, "The Teaching of Reading," 1937.
[2] "How Well Do You Read?" The Scribner Quiz, *Scribner's* Magazine, January, 1938, p. 88.
[3] *Thirty-Sixth Yearbook,* p. 15.

ple process which can be learned in the elementary school. The basic factors in the process include span of recognition, speed of perception, suppression of vocalization, and the like. The point of view that psychologically reading is not a complicated situation, but rather that efficient reading depends on the mastery of certain basic factors, which are probably few in number, is presented by Buswell in *How Adults Read*. Buswell further states: "There is evidence to indicate that systems of remedial instruction are becoming so complicated and detailed that they present an impossible obstacle to the improvement of reading." [4]

A second approach, exemplified by some of Thorndike's[5] writings, is that reading a paragraph is like solving a problem. It is an intricate process, consisting of ability to use knowledge of words and constructions and to understand sentences and paragraphs, the limits of which are set by an individual's intelligence. Some individuals will learn to read well without much training and others will never be able to read well. Thorndike[6] has also stated that he believes that the stimulation of life in general and the school studies other than reading will bring nearly to a maximum a given child's ability in this process.

Another approach is that reading is made up of numerous skills and techniques, the kind and quality of which vary with the purposes of the reader and with the reading situation. Lists, such as Horn and McBroom,[7] of specific reading skills illustrate the complexity of the reading situation. Others[8] indicate some of the life situations in which reading abilities are used and give an insight into the variety of purposes for which people read.

From the point of view of this approach, reading is a continu-

---

[4] Buswell, Guy Thomas, *How Adults Read*, p. 144, 1937.
[5] Thorndike, E. L., "Reading Is Reasoning: A Study of Mistakes in Paragraph Reading," *Journal of Educational Psychology*, Vol. VIII, June, 1917.
Thorndike, E. L., "Improving the Ability to Read," *Teachers College Record*, Vol. 36, Oct., Nov., Dec., 1934.
[6] *Ibid.*, p. 16.
[7] Horn, E. and McBroom, Maude, "A Survey of a Course of Study in Reading," Extension Bulletin No. 93, *College of Education Series* No. 3, University of Iowa, 1924.
[8] McKee, Paul, *Reading and Literature in the Elementary School*, pp. 48-55, 1934.
Hathaway, Gladys M., "Purposes for Which People Read," *University of Pittsburgh School of Education Journal*, Vol. 4, p. 83, 1929.

ous and tremendously important as well as very complex process, and while the emphasis upon the learning of reading skills remains in the elementary school, there is a recognized need for the acquisition of new reading skills and for the improvement of existing skills at every level of school life. The majority of investigations seem to support this view.

Because children encounter new reading activities in each new subject at every level,[9] it becomes desirable to provide specific instruction in the desired reading techniques and skills. And not only is this so, but in addition, provision should be made for diagnosis of the reading difficulties of a given child and for remedial instruction, since extreme individual differences exist in reading ability, considered as a whole, as well as in various aspects of that ability.

In an analysis of the reading of fifty ninth grade children, who were examined in the Educational Clinic at Northwestern University, a wide variety of specific deficiencies were found to exist.[10] Failure to acquire one or more of the many techniques or skills involved in reading is believed to be a frequent source of difficulty in reading.[11] Anderson[12] states that there is not a general reading ability acquired once and for all time to a sufficient degree to meet all needs of the reader. A good reader in one type of reading is likely to be a good reader in other types, but there are many exceptions.

Tentative minimum reading essentials, however, have been indicated for pupils entering grades four and seven. Lee[13] found that a grade score in silent reading of 4.0 is essential to satisfactory achievement in the intermediate grades. She compared children's reading ability with their actual achievement in arithmetic, spelling, language, social studies, etc., and what they were capable of doing as measured by an intelligence test, and found

[9] McCallister, James M., *Remedial and Corrective Instruction in Reading*, 1936.

[10] Witty, Paul A., "Diagnosis and Remedial Treatment of Reading Difficulties in the Secondary School," *Educational Trends*, Vol. 3, April, 1934.

[11] Gates, Arthur I., *The Improvement of Reading*, p. 12, 1935.

[12] Anderson, E. M., *Individual Differences in the Reading Ability of College Students*, p. 53, 1928.

[13] Lee, Dorris May, *The Importance of Reading for Achieving in Grades Four, Five, and Six*, 1933.

reading to be an important determiner of successful achievement. Gray[14] has stated: "Unpublished studies made in various schools show clearly that a grade score in silent reading of 7.0 or better is essential if pupils are able to engage successfully in the reading activities normally required at the junior-high-school level."

Despite the setting of minimum essentials of reading and despite the volume of material written on the subject, relatively little is known about the degree to which skill in the various aspects of reading determines scholastic achievement. The need arises for studies of the actual status of the reading skills possessed by students at various levels and of the relationships between these skills and achievement. In any such study, differences in intelligence must be measured and account taken of them. It has been difficult heretofore to get at this problem on the high school level because the non-verbal intelligence tests for those age ranges were not entirely satisfactory and because verbal tests of intelligence were also not satisfactory since they themselves are in effect reading tests. With the publication of the 1937 Revision of the Stanford-Binet Test of Intelligence[15] an acceptable instrument became available.

The investigation here reported was initiated for the purpose of determining the relationship between various reading skills and scholastic achievement in various subject matter areas on the ninth grade level.

[14] *Thirty-Sixth Yearbook*, p. 75.
[15] Terman, Lewis M. and Merrill, Maud A., *Measuring Intelligence*, 1937.

CHAPTER II

PROCEDURE

Population

THIS INVESTIGATION was carried on in the John Simpson Junior High School at Mansfield, Ohio. The population consisted of all the children in the 9A group (second half of the ninth grade). In the final statistical analyses, 300 of the 334 pupils who were enrolled in grade 9A during the semester were included; the others were dropped either because they withdrew from school or because it was impossible to gather complete data about them. This 9A group may be considered representative in regard to social and economic status since Mansfield is a typical mid-western industrial city and since children of this age level are not sent to private schools. The procedure followed in the school system is to promote the children at the end of each year so that each grade is relatively homogeneous with respect to chronological age.[1]

Tests Used in the Investigation

A tabulation of the tests used is given in Table I. The 1937 Revision of the Stanford-Binet Test of Intelligence, Form L, was administered in every case by the investigator. A graph of the distribution of the intelligence quotients of the 334 ninth grade children of this study is shown in Figure I which appears on the following page.

During the week of May 24, 1937, Cooperative Achievement Tests were administered by the classroom teachers with the exception of the Cooperative English Test, which was given by the investigator. Each child took four major subjects during the school year 1936–37. Achievement tests were given in only those

[1] Bond, Elden A., "A Method of Selecting Sub-normal Children for a Vocational School," *Journal of Juvenile Research,* July, 1937.

5

subjects for which Cooperative Achievement Tests were available.[2]

The subjects for which no test was given were shop, bookkeeping, and commerce and industry, which constitute approximately one-fourth of the total major subjects taken. The achievement

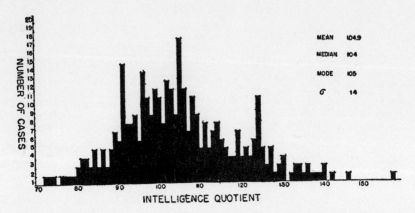

FIGURE I. Distribution of Intelligence Quotients of 334 Ninth Grade Children on the Stanford-Binet Test of Intelligence, Form L, 1937 Revision

of each child was measured in literary acquaintance, English, and either algebra or general mathematics. In addition, the achievement of all who took general science and Latin was also measured.

The Cooperative Achievement Tests used in this investigation will be discussed individually in the following paragraphs.

COOPERATIVE ENGLISH TEST

The Cooperative English Test, Form 1937, requires 80 minutes of testing time and affords a broad measure of a student's

[2] In a discussion of achievement tests, Strang comments on the Cooperative Achievement Tests as follows: "The high point, at present, in the construction of achievement tests on the high-school and college levels, is represented by the work of the Cooperative Test Service. This test construction laboratory has surveyed each field to be covered, constructed questions based on important content in the field, and attained a high degree of mechanical and statistical efficiency in making the tests valid and reliable and in establishing adequate norms." Strang, Ruth, *Behavior and Background of Students in College and Secondary School*, p. 171, 1937.

mastery of the basic principles of English. It provides a measure of three aspects of English achievement, namely, English usage, spelling, and vocabulary.

The vocabulary section, testing time 20 minutes, consists of

TABLE I

Tests Used in the Investigation

Test	Author	Publisher	Date of Copyright	Reliability	Testing Time (Minutes)
READING TESTS					
Iowa Silent Reading Test Form B (Revised) High Schools & Colleges	H. A. Greene A. N. Jorgensen V. H. Kelley	World Book	1931	.95*	35
Shank Tests of Reading Comprehension, Test II Form A, Grades 7, 8, 9	Spencer Shank	C. A. Gregory	1929	.903†	20
Traxler Silent Reading Form I, for Grades 7 to 10	Arthur E. Traxler	Public School Publishing	1934	.908‡	46
INTELLIGENCE TEST					
Stanford - Binet Test of Intelligence, Form L	Maud Merrill Lewis Terman	Houghton- Mifflin	1937	.982 to .898¶	Individual
		(¶Derived separately for various IQ levels)			

ACHIEVEMENT TESTS

1937 Cooperative Achievement Tests, Revised Series: Form N, Cooperative Test Service.

	Authors	Testing Time
English	S. A. Leonard, V. A. C. Henmon E. F. Lindquist, W. W. Cook M. F. Carpenter, D. G. Paterson F. S. Beers, G. Spaulding	80
Literary Acquaintance	F. S. Beers, D. G. Paterson G. B. Shepley	40
General Science	O. E. Underhill, S. R. Powers	40
Elementary Algebra	J. A. Long, L. P. Siceloff	40
General Mathematics	H. T. Lundholm, L. P. Siceloff	40
Latin	W. L. Carr, G. R. Humphries	40

* *Iowa Silent Reading Manual of Directions*, p. 6.
† *Student Responses in the Measurement of Reading Comprehension*, p. 54.
‡ *Teachers Handbook for Traxler Silent Reading Test*, p. 9.
¶ *Measuring Intelligence*, p. 46.

one hundred words, each followed by five words from which the student selects the one which most nearly corresponds in meaning to the tested word. This section offers a reliable measure of a student's ability to make fine discriminations in the meaning of words. Fifty-one of the one hundred words in this test of vocabulary are outside of Thorndike's 20,000 word list[3] and all but seven of the remaining fall within the 15,000 to 20,000 group.

The spelling section, requiring 10 minutes of testing time, consists of fifty groups of four words, one of which in most of the cases is misspelled. The student detects the misspelled words. The words are all found in Thorndike's 20,000 word list and the misspelled ones include the common spelling errors.

The usage part of the English test includes a section, requiring 10 minutes of testing time, which tests the ability of a student to select the most coherent sentence from a group of four; twenty of such groups make up the section. A second part of the usage test, requiring 15 minutes, is composed of twenty sentences in which the student makes suggested changes in the structure of each sentence. The usage test also includes two short proofreading selections, requiring 25 minutes of testing time, in which errors in punctuation, capitalization, and grammatical usage are to be detected and corrected.

LITERARY ACQUAINTANCE TEST

The Cooperative Literary Acquaintance Test, Form 1937, requires 40 minutes of testing time and contains 150 multiple-choice items selected on the basis of difficulty, discriminating quality, and proportionate representation of different fields and writers, and provides a comprehensive measure of an individual's acquaintance with the field of literature.

COOPERATIVE LATIN TEST

The Cooperative Latin Test, Elementary Form N, 1937, requires 40 minutes of testing time, and emphasizes functional

---

[3] Thorndike, E. L., *A Teacher's Word Book of the Twenty Thousand Words Found Most Frequently and Widely in General Reading for Children and Young People*, 1931.

knowledge of Latin rather than mere memorization of forms or rules. Part I consists of reading three paragraphs of Latin material and answering seven questions in English about each paragraph. Part II lists fifty Latin words, each followed by five English words, from which the student selects the one which most nearly corresponds to the specific Latin word. Part III is composed of 35 English sentences followed by an incomplete Latin translation, which the student completes by inserting one of five words or phrases.

COOPERATIVE ALGEBRA TEST

The Cooperative Algebra Test, Revised Series, Form N, consists of fifty-four short questions covering the application of the basic skills and principles included in elementary algebra. The student is asked to select from five the correct answer to each question; an illustration of one follows:

What is the product of -2 and -20?
(1) -40 (2) -10 (3) $+40$ (4) $+10$ (5) -22

COOPERATIVE GENERAL MATHEMATICS TEST

The Cooperative General Mathematics Test for High School Classes, Revised Series, Form N, 1937, is made up of sixty questions selected from materials incorporated in typical high school mathematics courses.

COOPERATIVE GENERAL SCIENCE TEST

The Cooperative General Science Test, Revised Series, Form N, 1937, includes 80 questions which afford a measure of how well informed students are concerning scientific developments that are usually stressed in a high school general science course. Reading of diagrams and figures as well as verbal questions is required.

READING TESTS

The reading tests were administered by the investigator during the same week the achievement tests were given. They provide measures of the following reading abilities.

COMPOSITE READING COMPREHENSION

The total comprehension score on the Iowa B, Traxler, and Shank reading tests were combined into a composite comprehension score by adding the sigma scores of each. The reliabilities of the comprehension scores, reported by the authors of the tests in the manuals of directions, are as follows: Iowa B, .95; Traxler, .926; Shank, .903.

A discussion of the measures of reading ability in the composite measure of reading comprehension will be presented in the following paragraphs.

The Iowa Silent Reading Test, Advanced Test, Form B (Revised) is made up of twelve sub-tests, each of which requires from $1\frac{1}{2}$ to 5 minutes of testing time. The total comprehension score includes the score received on word, paragraph, and sentence meaning, organization, and location of information sub-tests. With the exception of seven, all of the words in the test are in Thorndike's list of the 20,000 commonest words. In the first sub-test the student is required to read four paragraphs on the subject of "Rubber" and then answer fifteen questions on the material. Five minutes is allowed. Three stanzas of the poem "To Autumn" by John Keats, which the student reads and upon which he then answers fifteen questions, constitute the second sub-test. Next follows four vocabulary tests on social science, science, mathematics, and English. Forty-four of the seventy words in these tests are found in the 10,000 commonest words listed by Thorndike. The sub-test which measures the ability to comprehend the meaning of a sentence is made up of forty short sentences to be answered by either yes or no. The other sub-tests will be discussed later in this chapter.

The Traxler Silent Reading Test is made up of three parts, which provide measures of story and paragraph comprehension, and word meaning. Thirty-eight of the fifty words in the vocabulary test are from the 10,000 commonest words listed by Thorndike; the remaining twelve are found in the 10,000 to 20,000 group. The story, which the child reads and upon which he answers ten multiple-choice questions, is a relatively simple narrative about the life of a mother bear and her cub.

The Shank Reading Test consists of ten short paragraphs which the child reads and about which he answers seven different types of questions. The total comprehension score represents the child's general ability to comprehend the meaning of the material read. The material is relatively simple narrative; none of the words are outside Thorndike's list of the 20,000 commonest words.

A subjective classification[4] of the materials included in the composite reading comprehension score (which is based upon 99 minutes of testing time), in terms of minutes spent, is as follows:

Approximately 23 minutes are devoted to reading material which deals predominately with the field of social science. In this classification is included material on economics, history, and geography of the type devoted to artificial boundaries, names of cities, countries, etc.

Approximately 35 minutes are devoted to reading material predominately literary in nature, of which a large proportion is testing of vocabulary knowledge (not included under other headings).

Approximately 36 minutes are devoted to material predominately scientific in nature. The time devoted to the simple narrative on animal life (Part I of the Traxler test) was equally divided in this classification between the scientific and literary categories.

Approximately 5 minutes are devoted to mathematical material.

In order to illustrate the classification procedure, the following four items are quoted with the classification category:

[4] These breakdowns were made as a result of a conference between three people, one trained in mathematics, one in science, and the third in English and economics. The striking fact which developed from this conference is that the relatively simple materials such as are included in these tests have ramifications and implications in many different fields. In the case of much of the material, the one trained in science saw the scientific implications and classified it as predominately scientific; whereas the one trained in economics classified it as belonging in the social science area. In such instances, the decision of category was made after a careful group consideration of the specific item.

Item	*Category*
1. Boilers *emit* steam.	Scientific
2. *Defer* the payment.	Mathematical
3. A sad *epitaph*.	Literary
4. *Usury* is forbidden.	Social Scientific

POWER OF COMPREHENSION

Part III of the Traxler test provides a measure of ability to read materials of varying levels of difficulty. The element of time is largely eliminated, 20 minutes being allowed for the reading of six short paragraphs and the answering of twenty questions. The published reliability of the power of comprehension measure is .728. Three of the six paragraphs are classified as predominately scientific in content, one, literary, and two, social scientific.

LOCATION OF INFORMATION

The ability to locate information is measured by ten questions to be looked up in a selection from an index and twenty short questions, followed by seven words or phrases from which three key words are to be selected. The published reliability of this measure (sub-test 5 of the Iowa B) is .80. The inadvisability of using scores on a short five-minute sub-test such as this and the limitation of findings and interpretations based upon such a test are recognized. The five minutes of testing time are divided as follows: 3.2 minutes to material predominately of a social science content; 1.4 minutes to scientific material; and .4 minutes to literary material.

PARAGRAPH ORGANIZATION

The measure of ability to organize a paragraph is based upon scores received on Test 3 of the Iowa B battery. The published reliability of this measure is .86. Here again the limitations of findings and interpretations based upon a short sub-test of this kind are recognized. One section of this test consists of nine short paragraphs which the student reads and, from a list of five, selects one descriptive phrase that tells the central idea of the paragraph. The words and concepts are all relatively simple. The other section is made up of five paragraphs which the student outlines. The six minutes of testing time is divided as follows: 2.2 minutes to organizing material predominately from the field of social science; 3.5 minutes to scientific material; and .3 minutes to literary material.

COMPOSITE RATE

The Traxler Rate test is so arranged that the measure of rate is begun after the child has read three lines of the story about animal life and has had an opportunity to become interested in it. The time interval for this nature lore material, organized in the form of a running narrative, is 200 seconds.

Simple questions, which supposedly do not interfere with the rate of reading, are interspersed in the Iowa rate test. The students read, for two minutes, material upon the influence of the press in a democracy, answering questions as they go along. This material is set up in the form of a simple exposition.

There is some question about combining these two measures of speed of reading and giving them equal weight. It is possible that the running narrative material provides a better measure of speed of reading simple literary material. In spite of this, the two tests were combined so that the composite rate score might be based upon five and one-third minutes of testing time.

FIFTH GRADE MEASURE OF READING COMPREHENSION

In May, 1933, when the children in this group were in grade five, the short form of the Modern School Achievement Test was administered to them. A level of reading comprehension measure was available for 205 of the 300 children in the population. It was decided to determine the value this measure of reading comprehension might have in predicting scholastic achievement in grade nine.

This reading test of the Modern School Achievement Test is made up of 34 short paragraphs, from each of which two or three words are omitted and the child selects from a group of four words the word to insert in the blank space. Thirty minutes is allowed for reading the thirty-four paragraphs of varying degrees of difficulty.

FIFTH GRADE MEASURE OF READING SPEED

The speed of reading at the end of grade five was also available from the Modern School Achievement Test for the same 205 children. This five-minute test consists of fifty short paragraphs of about upper second or low third grade level of comprehension. Each paragraph contains a question, which is answered by selecting the correct word from a group of four.

STATISTICAL METHOD

The purpose of this study is to determine the existence of group relationships between various reading skills and various aspects of scholastic achievement. It does not attempt to develop predictive equations for such achievement, or to determine the reliability with which individual predictions can be made. The latter is an obvious next step, which it is practical to attempt only after group relationships have been shown to exist.

To compare the achievement of good and poor readers, some method of controlling differences in extraneous factors such as mental and chronological ages was needed. To have matched the good and poor readers on these background traits, either matching them person for person or group for group, would have resulted in a great reduction in the number of cases available and would also have produced groups not typical of the population of good and poor readers. The technique[5] employed is an adaptation of the method of analysis of variance which permits the retention of all or practically all the cases, comparisons being made within homogeneous subgroups, and then combined into a single index for all such subgroups. The analysis also could have been made by the use of residuals from a regression equation predicting achievement from the background traits, the mean residuals thus obtained for the two groups being compared. Either the method

[5] Johnson, Palmer O. and Neyman, Jerzy, "Tests of Certain Linear Hypotheses and Their Application to Some Educational Problems," *Statistical Research Memoirs*, I, 1936, 57–93.

used here or the study of such mean residuals can be made to yield a statement concerning the reliability of a mean difference to furnish evidence for group but not for individual prediction.*

The statistical method will be described step by step in the following pages:

1. In order that groups internally homogeneous with respect to one or more background traits could be compared, categories were set up. The background traits, which it was desirable to hold constant, were mental age and chronological age. The 300 cases were divided into six approximately equal mental age divisions and four chronological age divisions. Twenty-four categories resulted from the combination of the mental age and chronological age divisions. A master array was made by tabulating each of the 300 cases in the mental-chronological age category to which it belonged. Mental age and chronological age were held constant in this manner throughout the study.

2. The cases within a given category were ranked on the basis of a specific reading skill and were divided into three groups on the basis of this ranking. Whenever the number of cases within a given category was not exactly divisible by three, the remaining one or two cases were included in the middle group. The comparisons were made between the upper third and the lower third within a given category. The good reader group for the specific reading skill consisted of the totals of the one-third best readers within each of the twenty-four categories. Likewise, the poor reader group was made up of the totals of the one-third poorest readers within each of the twenty-four categories. The middle third in reading ability within each category was not used in the statistical analysis. This procedure was followed so that comparisons could be made between groups definitely separated in reading ability and presumably not separated in any other background trait. Any differences between the two groups with respect to scholastic achievement could be properly attributed

---

* Later the writer hopes to present evidence concerning the extent to which various reading tests, either singly or in combination with other tests and with other background traits, can be used to predict achievement in various school subjects. Such a study will employ very different methods from those used in the present study, and it was not feasible to combine the two undertakings.

either to chance sampling effects or to the fact that the reading skill was a factor in achievement.

A master array of this type was made up for each of the seven reading skills investigated.

3. Working sheets for use in the statistical analyses were made for each of the measures of achievement by recording a given score in the specific category and the reading group to which each case belonged.

Two categories and the summation of the 24 categories of the literary acquaintance working sheet are shown in Table II; the good and poor reader groups were composed of the upper third and lower third in each category with respect to ability in reading comprehension.

The calculations for each category were as follows:

	Good Readers	Poor Readers
Number of Cases	N_x	N_y
Sum of the Scores	ΣX	ΣY
Sum of the Squares	ΣX^2	ΣY^2
Mean	$\overline{X}$	$\overline{Y}$

Step I. The following calculations were made for each category:

$$\overline{X} - \overline{Y}$$

$$\frac{N_x N_y}{N_x + N_y}$$

$$\frac{(\Sigma X + \Sigma Y)^2}{N_x + N_y}$$

$$(\Sigma X^2 + \Sigma Y^2) - \frac{(\Sigma X + \Sigma Y)^2}{N_x + N_y}$$

$$\frac{(\overline{X} - \overline{Y})\, N_x N_y}{N_x + N_y}$$

(In the calculations thus far the summations were for the number of cases within each category. When the calculations for each category have been completed it is necessary to combine the results for all categories. It should be noticed that the summation signs from this point on were run over all the categories, whereas the summations in the previous calculations were only for the cases within a category.)

TABLE II

SECTION OF THE WORK SHEET OF THE RELATIONSHIP BETWEEN COMPOSITE READING COMPREHENSION AND LITERARY ACQUAINTANCE

Group	Mental Age 195–214		Summation of the 24 Categories
	Chronological Age		
	176–180	181–185	
Good Reader Groups	21	6	
	19	17	
	17	27	
	19	36	
	24		
	31		
	18		
	36		
N_x	8	4	93
ΣX	185	86	1605
ΣX^2	4609	2350	34847
$\overline{X}$ (Mean)	23.1	21.5	
	10	10	
	8	17	
	7	17	
	8	12	
Poor Reader Groups	14		
	15		
	14		
	11		
N_y	8	4	93
ΣY	87	56	864
ΣY^2	1015	822	11908
$\overline{Y}$ (Mean)	10.9	14.0	
$\overline{X} - \overline{Y}$	12.2	7.5	
$N_x N_y \div (N_x + N_y)$	4.0	2.0	46.5
$(\Sigma X + \Sigma Y)^2 \div (N_x + N_y)$	4624.0	2520.0	36918.4
$(\Sigma X^2 + \Sigma Y^2) - \dfrac{(\Sigma X + \Sigma Y)^2}{N_x + N_y}$	1000.0	652.0	9836.6
$(\overline{X} - \overline{Y}) \dfrac{N_x N_y}{N_x + N_y}$	48.8	15.0	370.3

Step II. The following summations were made for the twenty-four categories:

$$\Sigma \frac{N_x N_y}{N_x + N_y}$$

$$\Sigma(\Sigma X^2 + \Sigma Y^2) - \frac{(\Sigma X + \Sigma Y)^2}{N_x + N_y}$$

$$\Sigma\frac{(\overline{X} - \overline{Y})\, N_x N_y}{N_x + N_y}$$

(Since Y is the poor reader group, when $\Sigma\dfrac{(\overline{X} - \overline{Y})\, N_x N_y}{N_x + N_y}$ is negative, the relationship is in favor of the poor readers. The direction of the difference does not influence the comparison. It is conceivable to have a highly significant ratio when the difference is in favor of the poor readers.)

Step III. Calculations based on the following formulas were made:

$$S_b{}^2 = \frac{\left\{ \Sigma(\overline{X} - \overline{Y})\dfrac{N_x N_y}{N_x + N_y} \right\}^2}{\Sigma\dfrac{N_x N_y}{N_x + N_y}}$$

$S_b{}^2$ = Mean variance between the good and poor reader groups.
r = Number of relations tested, which in this case is 1.

$$S_a{}^2 = \Sigma\left\{ (\Sigma X^2 + \Sigma Y^2) - \frac{(\Sigma X + \Sigma Y)^2}{N_x + N_y} \right\} - S_b{}^2$$

$S_a{}^2$ = Mean variance within the good and poor reader groups
n = Number of cases
s = Number of categories
F = Ratio of the larger mean variance to the smaller mean variance.

$$F = \frac{S_b{}^2(N - S - 1)}{S_a{}^2(r)}$$

Step IV. The z score of the ratio of the greater mean variance to the smaller mean variance was calculated by finding one-half the natural logarithm of the ratio (F).

The z score was then compared with Fisher's[6] table of the distribution of z to ascertain the probability of exceeding the observed z value by chance in random samples of like populations.

The greater mean variance was not always the variance between the good and poor reader groups. In some instances, especially with regard to the fast and slow reader groups, the greater

[6] Fisher, R. A., *Statistical Methods for Research Workers*, Table VI, 1936.

mean variance was the variance within the groups and it was necessary to invert the fraction before the ratio could be obtained, as a z score may never be negative. A much larger z score would have had to result in these cases before it could have been judged to be significant since the larger number of degrees of freedom was associated with the larger mean variance.

The calculations indicated by the formulas given above may be illustrated by using the summations arrived at in Table II as an example.

$$S_b^2 = \frac{(370.3)^2}{46.5} = 2948.9$$

$$S_a^2 = 9836.6 - 2948.9 = 6887.7$$

$$F = \frac{2948.9\,(186 - 24 - 1)}{6887.7\,(1)} = 68.9$$

TABLE III

RELATIONSHIP BETWEEN COMPOSITE READING COMPREHENSION AND LITERARY ACQUAINTANCE

ANALYSIS OF VARIANCE
BASIC MATCHING CRITERIA: MENTAL AGE AND CHRONOLOGICAL AGE

Source of Variation	Degrees of Freedom	Mean Variance	Ratio	z	P
Between Groups	1	2948.9			
Within Groups	161	42.8	68.9	2.12	$P < .001$

Here we are testing whether one estimate of variance, 2948.9, derived from 1 degree of freedom, is significantly greater than a second such estimate, 42.8, derived from 161 degrees of freedom. The ratio of the greater mean variance to the smaller mean variance is 68.9. A comparison of the z score of this ratio, 2.12, with Fisher's[7] table of the distribution of z shows that a value as large as the observed value could be expected to occur by chance in less than .1 per cent of random samples of like populations. We have thus established the fact that a highly sig-

[7] *Ibid*, Table VI.

nificant relationship exists between skill in composite reading comprehension and literary acquaintance on the ninth grade level. In other words, those students, in general, who have achieved skill in reading comprehension, when inequalities due to differences in mental and chronological age are eliminated, have a better chance of being successful in ninth grade literary acquaintance than students of lesser skill in reading comprehension.

PICTORIAL PRESENTATION OF RELATIONSHIPS

In order to represent in pictorial fashion some of the relationships, three dimensional graphs were drawn. These were constructed in the following fashion:

(1) A specific reading skill distribution was divided into twelve equal steps.

(2) The IQ distribution was divided into twelve equal steps.

(3) Achievement scores in a specific subject were recorded in the IQ and reading skill block to which each case belonged.

(4) A mean achievement score was determined for each block.

(5) Drawings in perspective were made to show the curve of these mean scores.

CHAPTER III

ANALYSIS OF FINDINGS

IN THE INTERPRETATION of the relationships between skill in the various reading abilities and scholastic achievement in the various ninth grade subjects, it should be understood, of course, that inequalities exist due to differences in mental age and chronological age. In order to obtain relevant relationships, such inequalities were eliminated by the method of matching whereby groups of approximately the same mental and chronological age were compared. This method was used in all of the statistical work.

COMPOSITE READING COMPREHENSION

The analysis of the variance in scholastic achievement of two groups, separated on the basis of reading comprehension ability, is given in Table IV. Reading comprehension ability was determined by combining the sigma scores of the total comprehension scores on the Traxler, Shank, and Iowa B reading tests. Explanation of the statistical procedure is given in Chapter II, pages 14-20.

Column 5 of Table IV indicates the probability of obtaining samples as large as the observed values of z. In the case of achievement in English, the probability of a value as large as the observed value occurring by chance is less than .1 per cent in random samples of like populations. This is a highly significant relationship statistically. Children who obtain high scores in these reading comprehension tests will on the average show higher scholastic achievement in English than children who obtain low scores on these tests of reading comprehension. The relationships between reading comprehension and achievement in the three separate measures of English are also highly significant as shown by the fact that the probabilities are less than .1 per cent. Reading comprehension is a highly significant factor in literary acquaintance, just as it is in the other measures of achievement in English, as shown by the fact that P is less than .1 per cent.

TABLE IV

RELATIONSHIP BETWEEN READING COMPREHENSION AND NINTH GRADE ACHIEVEMENT

ANALYSIS OF VARIANCE

BASIC MATCHING CRITERIA: MENTAL AGE AND CHRONOLOGICAL AGE

Source of Variation	Degrees of Freedom	Mean Variance	Ratio	z	P
English Achievement					
Between Groups	1	45878.5			
Within Groups	161	406.9	112.8	2.36	P < .001
English Usage					
Between Groups	1	12025.9			
Within Groups	161	198.0	60.7	2.05	P < .001
Spelling					
Between Groups	1	1057.0			
Within Groups	161	48.7	21.7	1.54	P < .001
Vocabulary					
Between Groups	1	5556.3			
Within Groups	161	57.8	96.2	2.28	P < .001
Literary Acquaintance					
Between Groups	1	2948.9			
Within Groups	161	42.8	68.9	2.12	P < .001
General Science					
Between Groups	1	373.0			
Within Groups	68	45.1	8.3	1.06	.001 < P < .01
Algebra					
Between Groups	1	261.9			
Within Groups	43	40.7	6.4	0.93	.01 < P < .05
General Mathematics					
Between Groups	1	18.3			
Within Groups	84	15.7	1.2	0.09	.05 < P
Latin					
Between Groups	1	1809.6			
Within Groups	36	153.1	11.8	1.23	.001 < P < .01
Composite Achievement					
Between Groups	1	423.3			
Within Groups	47	36.0	11.8	1.23	.001 < P < .01

This measure of reading comprehension includes a broad sampling of reading abilities, the material for which is drawn from several subject matter areas. The fact that approximately one-third of the material in the reading tests is predominately literary in content may tend to increase the relationships. Two of the reading tests include sub-tests on knowledge of vocabulary, as does the English achievement test. Although there are vocabulary items in the intelligence test, it was so constructed to keep verbal items at a minimum, and the effect of varying degrees of intelligence has been held constant by the statistical procedure. The reading tests sample many reading abilities in addition to knowledge of vocabulary. The English acheivement tests include much material that is quite different from the literary content of the reading tests. These very high relationships indicate many common elements. We are not, in effect, comparing a comprehension test in English with a comprehension test in English. On the contrary, these data point rather conclusively to the fact that in order to achieve in a ninth grade English course it is highly desirable that a pupil should read with a high degree of reading comprehension.

ACHIEVEMENT IN GENERAL SCIENCE

One hundred sixty-three of the 300 children in this study were enrolled in classes in general science. The number in the good reader group on the basis of reading comprehension was 50, while there were 37 in the poor reader group. The observed value lies between the values for $P = .1$ per cent and $P = 1$ per cent. A value as large as the observed value would be expected to occur by chance in less than 1 per cent of random samples of like populations. The relationship between ability in reading comprehension and scholastic achievement in ninth grade general science may be judged to be a highly significant one. Children who have high ability in reading comprehension will show, on the average, higher scholastic achievement in general science than children who have low ability in reading comprehension. More of the content of the reading tests was drawn from the field of science than from any other subject matter area. However, the concepts and vocabulary load of the reading test material appear to be at a lower level than in the general science achievement test. The similarity of the material included in the tests of the two factors here considered undoubtedly accounts for a part of the relationship.

ACHIEVEMENT IN ALGEBRA AND IN GENERAL MATHEMATICS

One hundred nine of the 300 children in this study were enrolled in classes in algebra. The number in the good reader group on the basis of reading comprehension was 31, while there were 22 in the poor reader group. The observed value lies between the values for $P = 5$ per cent and $P = 1$ per cent. A value as large as the observed one would be expected to occur by chance in less than 5 per cent of random samples of like populations. This is probably a significant relationship statistically. It is likely that those children who have a high level of reading comprehension will, in general, have significantly higher scholastic achievement in algebra than the children who as a group have lower levels of reading comprehension.

One hundred eighty-one of the 300 children in the study were enrolled in courses in ninth grade general mathematics. The number falling in the good reader group was 44, while 61 were in the poor reader group. The observed value is less than that for $P = 5$ per cent, so the relationship is not significant.

Approximately 5 per cent (in terms of testing time) of the material included in the reading tests is mathematical in content. If a measure of reading comprehension of reading mathematical types of materials had been used instead of the composite measure of reading comprehension, the relationships might have been more significant.

ACHIEVEMENT IN LATIN

Eighty-eight of the 300 children were enrolled in courses in ninth grade Latin. The number falling in the good reader group on the basis of reading comprehension was 27, while there were 18 in the poor reader group. The observed value lies between the points of Fisher's distribution for $P = 1$ per cent and $P = .1$ per cent. Thus, a value as large as the observed one would be expected to occur by chance in less than 1 per cent of random samples of like populations. The relationship existing between reading comprehension and achievement in ninth grade Latin is a highly significant one. Those children who rank high in reading comprehension will in general have significantly better achievement in Latin than those children who rank low in reading comprehension.

COMPOSITE NINTH GRADE ACHIEVEMENT

One hundred of the 300 children in this study were enrolled in a college preparatory course. For this group, a measure of scholastic achievement in all four major subjects was available. Sigma scores of achievement in each subject were combined into a composite achievement score. There were 31 cases in each group. The observed value of the relationship between reading comprehension and achievement in the ninth grade college preparatory course lies between the points of Fisher's distribution of z for $P = 1$ per cent and $P = .1$ per cent. A value as large as the observed value would be expected to occur by chance in less than 1 per cent of random samples of like populations. Reading comprehension, when groups are matched on mental and chronological age, is a highly significant factor in scholastic achievement in the ninth grade college preparatory course.

Every classification tabulated in Table IV shows more variation between groups than within groups, although in the case of one classification, namely, general mathematics, the ratio is not reliable. A word of caution should be interpolated at this point. Errors of measurement would tend to increase the variance within the groups and thus decrease the significance of the variation between the groups. It is important to remember, too, that in the case of some of these classifications the groups were rather small. When groups are small, a very real difference may not be revealed as significant. The effect of the unreliability of measurement and the unreliability of sampling upon the variance ratios should be held in mind in the following discussions.

The importance of ability in reading comprehension, as here measured, to achievement in the various ninth grade subjects, with the exception of achievement in general mathematics, when age and intelligence are held constant, has been clearly indicated by these data.

POWER OF COMPREHENSION

The analysis of the variance in scholastic achievement of two groups separated on the basis of power of comprehension is presented in Table V. Explanation of the statistical procedure is given in Chapter II, pages 14-20. The power of comprehension score of Part III of the Traxler Silent Reading Test provides a

TABLE V

RELATIONSHIP BETWEEN POWER OF READING COMPREHENSION AND NINTH GRADE ACHIEVEMENT

ANALYSIS OF VARIANCE
BASIC MATCHING CRITERIA: MENTAL AGE AND CHRONOLOGICAL AGE

Source of Variation	Degrees of Freedom	Mean Variance	Ratio	z	P
English Achievement					
Between Groups	1	24621.5			
Within Groups	161	442.7	55.6	2.01	P < .001
English Usage					
Between Groups	1	7075.6			
Within Groups	161	219.9	32.2	1.74	P < .001
Spelling					
Between Groups	1	641.4			
Within Groups	161	45.6	14.1	1.32	P < .001
Vocabulary					
Between Groups	1	2254.8			
Within Groups	161	49.7	45.3	1.91	P < .001
Literary Acquaintance					
Between Groups	1	1561.9			
Within Groups	161	38.6	40.4	1.85	P < .001
General Science					
Between Groups	1	475.4			
Within Groups	74	60.2	7.9	1.03	.001 < P < .01
Algebra					
Between Groups	1	220.1			
Within Groups	44	56.0	3.9	0.68	.05 < P
General Mathematics					
Within Groups	87	15.6			
Between Groups	1	14.7	1.1*	0.05	.05 < P
Latin					
Between Groups	1	182.9			
Within Groups	37	173.0	1.1	0.05	.05 < P
Composite Achievement					
Between Groups	1	302.7			
Within Groups	47	34.7	8.7	1.08	.001 < P < .01

* In favor of the poor readers.

measure of reading comprehension of material arranged in six paragraphs graduated in difficulty. Despite the fact that this test is relatively short, it provided a range in scores of from 6 to 40; Q_1 at 20; Md. at 26; Q_3 at 30.

This measure of reading comprehension is based upon the student's ability to read material of varying levels of difficulty, whereas the composite reading comprehension measure is based upon the student's ability in several reading skills.

ACHIEVEMENT IN ENGLISH

The relationships between this measure of power of comprehension and the various measures of achievement in English, including literary acquaintance, are all highly significant. The z values of the relationship existing between power of comprehension and each of the five different measures of achievement in English are all larger than the .1 per cent value and so would not be expected to occur in random sampling even in one out of a thousand trials. In view of these high relationships and in view of the fact that only one of the six paragraphs in the reading sub-test is predominately literary in content (the other five were taken from the fields of science and social science), there can be no doubt that level of reading comprehension is a factor in scholastic achievement in ninth grade English.

ACHIEVEMENT IN OTHER SUBJECTS

A highly significant relationship exists between power of comprehension and achievement in general science as shown by the fact that the observed value lies between the points for Fisher's distribution of z for $P = 1$ per cent and $P = .1$ per cent. Power of comprehension is definitely a factor in scholastic achievement in general science. This relationship may have been increased because of the fact that approximately one-half of the material included in the reading measure is scientific in content. The difference in variability in achievement in algebra, though suggestive of a real effect, cannot be judged significant on the basis of these data.

The observed difference in achievement in Latin between

groups separated on power of comprehension is not significant. In the case of achievement in general mathematics, not only is the difference reversed in sign, so that the mean achievement of the poor reader group was better than the mean achievement of the good reader group, and not only is the difference so small as to be explicable on the basis of random sampling, but also the variance between groups is less than the variance among members of the same group. This reversal of the ratio does not occur elsewhere in Table V.

A highly significant relationship exists between power of comprehension and composite achievement in the college preparatory course; that is, power of comprehension is definitely a factor in ninth grade composite achievement. This is shown by the fact that the observed value lies between the points in Fisher's distribution of z for $P = 1$ per cent and $P = .1$ per cent.

FIFTH GRADE LEVEL OF COMPREHENSION

Table VI presents an analysis of the variance in ninth grade comprehension as measured by the Short Form of the Modern School Achievement Test given when the children were in the fifth grade. Two hundred five of the children in the population took the Modern School Achievement Test in May, 1933. The analysis of Table VI follows the same procedure as that outlined in Chapter II, pages 14-20.

ACHIEVEMENT IN ENGLISH

In the case of achievement in English, the probability of a value as large as the observed value occurring by chance is less than .1 per cent. Thus the children who were among the one-third most skilled readers on the basis of level of comprehension in grade five were significantly better achievers, as a group, in English in grade nine than were the children who made up the one-third poorest readers, although the effects of mental and chronological age had been eliminated. The same relationships are shown to hold true with regard to the three aspects of English, namely, English usage, spelling, and vocabulary; this relationship, however, is more pronounced with regard to vocabulary. This

TABLE VI

RELATIONSHIP BETWEEN READING COMPREHENSION IN GRADE FIVE AND
NINTH GRADE ACHIEVEMENT

ANALYSIS OF VARIANCE
BASIC MATCHING CRITERIA: MENTAL AGE AND CHRONOLOGICAL AGE

Source of Variation	Degrees of Freedom	Mean Variance	Ratio	z	P
English Achievement					
Between Groups	1	13179.3			
Within Groups	113	555.3	23.7	1.58	P < .001
English Usage					
Between Groups	1	2107.7			
Within Groups	113	237.1	8.9	1.09	.001 < P < .01
Spelling					
Between Groups	1	557.7			
Within Groups	113	51.8	10.8	1.19	P < .001
Vocabulary					
Between Groups	1	2164.8			
Within Groups	113	67.0	32.3	1.74	P < .001
Literary Acquaintance					
Between Groups	1	724.0			
Within Groups	113	48.0	15.1	1.36	P < .001
General Science					
Between Groups	1	82.7			
Within Groups	50	65.3	1.3	0.13	.05 < P
Algebra					
Between Groups	1	100.6			
Within Groups	31	44.3	2.3	0.42	.05 < P
General Mathematics					
Within Groups	58	23.4			
Between Groups	1	1.1	21.3	1.53	.05 < P
Latin					
Within Groups	27	124.7			
Between Groups	1	69.9	1.8*	0.29	.05 < P
Composite Achievement					
Within Groups	35	34.8			
Between Groups	1	4.7	7.4	1.00	.05 < P

* In favor of the poor readers.

means, then, that children as a group who have achieved a high
level of comprehension in grade five should be expected to be
scholastically more successful in ninth grade English as a whole,
as well as in the three special aspects of ninth grade English, than
the group of children who have not reached those levels of reading comprehension. A highly significant relationship is likewise

shown between reading comprehension in grade five and literary acquaintance in grade nine.

It is interesting that a thirty-minute reading comprehension test given to children in the fifth grade, which was administered and scored by the classroom teachers, has real value in predicting scholastic success in the several phases of ninth grade English. It is well to remember, however, that this is a group prediction and not an individual one.

ACHIEVEMENT IN OTHER NINTH GRADE SUBJECTS

The relationships found to exist between the fifth grade measure of reading comprehension and the other measures of scholastic achievement in the ninth grade college preparatory course, cannot be judged significant on the basis of these data. The observed values are such as might occur in random samples of like populations. In the case of general mathematics, Latin, and composite achievement, the variance between groups is less than the variance among members of the same group.

LOCATION OF INFORMATION

The analysis of variance in scholastic achievement of two groups separated on the basis of skill in the use of an index is presented in Table VII. It should be remembered in considering the relationships between ability to locate information and scholastic achievement that that measure of ability is based upon five minutes of testing the selection of key words in a selection and the use of an index, as measured by sub-test 5 of the Iowa B test. This provides a measure of a work-study type of reading.

The relationships which exist between this work-study technique and achievement in English as a whole, in English usage, in vocabulary, in literary acquaintance, and in algebra are all highly significant. The probability in the case of all of these measures of achievement is that z values as large as the observed values would occur by chance in less than one random sample out of a thousand. The relationships which exist between ability to locate information and achievement in spelling, in general science, and in general mathematics are probably significant,

TABLE VII

RELATIONSHIP BETWEEN SKILL IN THE LOCATION OF INFORMATION AND
NINTH GRADE ACHIEVEMENT

ANALYSIS OF VARIANCE
BASIC MATCHING CRITERIA: MENTAL AGE AND CHRONOLOGICAL AGE

Source of Variation	Degrees of Freedom	Mean Variance	Ratio	z	P
English Achievement					
Between Groups	I	18134.9			
Within Groups	161	581.2	31.2	1.72	P < .001
English Usage					
Between Groups	I	9990.9			
Within Groups	161	218.8	45.7	1.91	P < .001
Spelling					
Between Groups	I	346.3			
Within Groups	161	58.2	5.9	0.89	.01 < P < .05
Vocabulary					
Between Groups	I	1046.5			
Within Groups	161	62.0	16.9	1.41	P < .001
Literary Acquaintance					
Between Groups	I	1332.3			
Within Groups	161	47.4	28.1	1.67	P < .001
General Science					
Between Groups	I	254.1			
Within Groups	70	49.2	5.2	0.82	.01 < P < .05
Algebra					
Between Groups	I	753.8			
Within Groups	45	47.4	15.9	1.38	P < .001
General Mathematics					
Between Groups	I	91.8			
Within Groups	89	17.1	5.4	0.84	.01 < P < .05
Latin					
Between Groups	I	443.6			
Within Groups	33	173.8	2.6	0.48	.05 < P
Composite Achievement					
Between Groups	I	294.0			
Within Groups	47	32.7	9.0	1.10	.001 < P < .01

since the observed values in the case of these three measures of achievement lie between the point in Fisher's distribution of z for $P = 5$ per cent and $P = 1$ per cent. In the case of general mathematics this work-study type of reading is the only one of the seven measures of reading skill which appears to be a factor in achievement.

The differences in variability in Latin achievement, though

suggestive of a real effect, cannot be judged significant on these data.

A highly significant relationship exists between skill in this work-study technique and composite achievement in the college preparatory course. The probability is that a value as large as the observed value would be expected to occur by chance in less than 1 per cent of random samples. The importance of reading in ninth grade achievement is well illustrated by the fact that groups separated on the basis of but five minutes of testing of reading ability show reading to be so significant a factor in achievement.

Paragraph Organization

The analysis of the variance in scholastic achievement of two groups separated on the basis of skill in paragraph organization is shown in Table VIII. Sub-test 3 of the Iowa Silent Reading Test requires 6 minutes of testing time and measures the ability to find the central thought in a paragraph and the ability to outline. The content of the material included in this sub-test is taken from the fields of science and social science, with the exception of one item which is from the field of literature. Here again, it should be remembered that this measure of reading is based upon a short sub-test, the validity of which is undetermined.

The differences in variability between skill in paragraph organization and achievement in English usage, vocabulary, literary acquaintance, and in total English are all highly significant. The relationships between paragraph organization and achievement in spelling, general science, algebra, general mathematics, Latin, and in composite achievement are all insignificant. Since over half of the content of the reading test is scientific, it might have been expected that a significant relationship would exist. The null hypothesis that skill in outlining is not important has been tested and the results have failed to cause the hypothesis to be rejected. The results indicate that differences of the magnitude of the observed values are not inconsistent with the hypothesis that the two groups are alike in the population. Thus skill in outlining scientific material and in selecting the central thought

TABLE VIII

RELATIONSHIP BETWEEN SKILL IN PARAGRAPH ORGANIZATION AND
NINTH GRADE ACHIEVEMENT

ANALYSIS OF VARIANCE
BASIC MATCHING CRITERIA: MENTAL AGE AND CHRONOLOGICAL AGE

Source of Variation	Degrees of Freedom	Mean Variance	Ratio	z	P
English Achievement					
Between Groups	1	6804.4			
Within Groups	161	526.9	12.9	1.28	P < .001
English Usage					
Between Groups	1	2695.0			
Within Groups	161	272.2	9.9	1.15	.001 < P < .01
Spelling					
Between Groups	1	88.9			
Within Groups	161	50.9	1.7	0.27	.05 < P
Vocabulary					
Between Groups	1	562.3			
Within Groups	161	58.6	9.6	1.13	.001 < P < .01
Literary Acquaintance					
Between Groups	1	412.5			
Within Groups	161	47.8	8.6	1.08	.001 < P < .01
General Science					
Within Groups	76	53.4			
Between Groups	1	0.6	89.0*	2.24	.05 < P
Algebra					
Between Groups	1	97.6			
Within Groups	45	47.5	2.1	0.37	.05 < P
General Mathematics					
Between Groups	1	41.3			
Within Groups	90	15.0	2.7*	0.50	.05 < P
Latin					
Within Groups	34	220.4			
Between Groups	1	153.1	1.4	0.17	.05 < P
Composite Achievement					
Between Groups	1	69.4			
Within Groups	47	40.8	1.7	0.27	.05 < P

* In favor of the poor readers.

of paragraphs predominately scientific in content, as here measured, has not been proved a factor in scholastic achievement in
general science. Other reading abilities, namely, composite comprehension, power of comprehension, and ability to locate information, are significant factors in scholastic achievement in
ninth grade general science, even though the content of the reading tests is not so predominately scientific.

In the case of general science and Latin, the variance within the groups is greater than the variance between groups, although in both cases the ratio is not reliable. And, also, in the case of general science and general mathematics, the difference is reversed in sign, the mean achievement of the poor reader group being better than the mean achievement of the good reader group.

Skill in paragraph organization, as measured by sub-test 3 of the Iowa test, is a significant factor in achievement in English, but has not been shown to be a factor in achievement in other ninth grade subjects.

SPEED OF READING

The analysis of the variance in scholastic achievement of two groups separated on the basis of a composite measure of speed of reading is presented in Table IX. The composite speed measure was determined by combining the sigma scores of reading speed on the Traxler and Iowa B tests. The Traxler rate test is based upon 200 seconds of reading a simple running narrative on animal life. The Iowa rate test consists of reading for two minutes a simple exposition of the "Influence of the Press" and answering several questions interspersed in the material.

ACHIEVEMENT IN ENGLISH

In the case of achievement in English, P is less than that given in Fisher's distribution of z for $P = 5$ per cent. Thus the relationship between speed of reading and achievement in English, when the effects of differences in mental and chronological age are eliminated, cannot be judged significant. However, speed of reading has a highly significant relationship to one part of achievement in ninth grade English, namely, size of vocabulary. The fast readers have significantly larger vocabularies as a group than the slow readers. The relationships between speed of reading and both English usage and spelling show more variation within groups than between groups, the variation, however, being such as might have been expected to arise by chance alone.

In the case of literary acquaintance, the probability of a score as large as the observed score occurring by chance is less than

TABLE IX

RELATIONSHIP BETWEEN READING SPEED AND NINTH GRADE ACHIEVEMENT X

ANALYSIS OF VARIANCE

BASIC MATCHING CRITERIA: MENTAL AGE AND CHRONOLOGICAL AGE

Source of Variation	Degrees of Freedom	Mean Variance	Ratio	z	P
English Achievement					
Between Groups	1	1126.0			
Within Groups	161	616.4	1.8	0.29	.05 < P
English Usage					
Within Groups	161	243.2			
Between Groups	1	5.1	49.6	1.95	.05 < P
Spelling					
Within Groups	161	49.5			
Between Groups	1	3.5	14.1*	1.32	.05 < P
Vocabulary					
Between Groups	1	706.1			
Within Groups	161	54.9	13.0	1.28	P < .001
Literary Acquaintance					
Between Groups	1	366.8			
Within Groups	161	49.0	7.5	1.01	.001 < P < .01
General Science					
Within Groups	78	61.0			
Between Groups	1	21.7	2.8*	0.51	.05 < P
Algebra					
Within Groups	44	55.7			
Between Groups	1	36.2	1.5*	0.20	.05 < P
General Mathematics					
Within Groups	88	14.5			
Between Groups	1	5.6	2.6*	0.48	.05 < P
Latin					
Within Groups	36	159.3			
Between Groups	1	81.1	2.0	0.35	.05 < P
Composite Achievement					
Between Groups	1	85.5			
Within Groups	47	38.1	2.2*	0.39	.05 < P

* In favor of the slow readers.

one in a hundred in random samples of like populations. Speed of reading may thus be judged to be a highly significant factor in literary acquaintance.

ACHIEVEMENT IN OTHER NINTH GRADE SUBJECTS

That none of the relationships between speed of reading and achievement in general science, algebra, general mathematics,

Latin, as well as composite achievement, is significant, is shown by the fact that the probabilities are such as might have been expected to arise by chance alone. It is noteworthy that the trend in the following measures of scholastic achievement is in favor of the slow reader groups: spelling, general science, algebra, general mathematics, and composite achievement. It is noteworthy, also, that the variance within groups is larger than the variance between groups in the case of general science, algebra, general mathematics, and Latin.

FIFTH GRADE SPEED OF READING

Table X presents an analysis of variance in ninth grade scholastic achievement of two groups separated on the basis of scores in reading speed received on the Short Form of the Modern School Achievement Test given when the children were in the fifth grade. A comparison of Tables IX and X shows that many of the same relationships which exist between ninth grade speed of reading and scholastic achievement hold with regard to fifth grade speed of reading and ninth grade scholastic achievement. For example, significant relationships exist between speed of reading and both word knowledge and literary acquaintance, while the relationships between speed of reading and the other measures of achievement in English are not significant. Also, the relationships between the fifth grade measure of speed and achievement in general science, algebra, and general mathematics are such as would have been expected to occur by chance alone. On the other hand, significant relationships in favor of the slow reader groups exist between speed of reading and both achievement in Latin and in composite achievement. Thus, when allowances are made for inequalities which exist in mental and chronological ages, the children in the slow reader group in grade five are at a significant advantage when they begin the study of Latin in the ninth grade. A similar relationship is shown to hold true with regard to composite ninth grade achievement.

The consistency of the reversals in mean variance, tabulated in Tables IV to X, is worthy of attention, even though the ratio in each case is not significant. In Table IV, reading comprehen-

TABLE X

RELATIONSHIP BETWEEN READING SPEED IN GRADE FIVE AND NINTH GRADE
ACHIEVEMENT

ANALYSIS OF VARIANCE
BASIC MATCHING CRITERIA: MENTAL AGE AND CHRONOLOGICAL AGE

Source of Variation	Degrees of Freedom	Mean Variance	Ratio	z	P
English Achievement					
Between Groups	1	2152.1			
Within Groups	113	583.6	3.7	0.66	.05 < P
English Usage					
Within Groups	113	245.3			
Between Groups	1	122.0	2.0	0.35	.05 < P
Spelling					
Between Groups	1	154.6			
Within Groups	113	60.0	2.6	0.48	.05 < P
Vocabulary					
Between Groups	1	361.1			
Within Groups	113	75.6	4.8	0.78	.01 < P < .05
Literary Acquaintance					
Between Groups	1	220.1			
Within Groups	113	45.2	4.9	0.79	.01 < P < .05
General Science					
Between Groups	1	137.6			
Within Groups	52	72.6	1.9*	0.32	.05 < P
Algebra					
Between Groups	1	53.6			
Within Groups	33	44.4	1.2*	0.09	.05 < P
General Mathematics					
Within Groups	53	22.3			
Between Groups	1	7.0	3.2	0.58	.05 < P
Latin					
Between Groups	1	594.0			
Within Groups	30	110.8	5.4*	0.84	.01 < P < .05
Composite Achievement					
Between Groups	1	150.3			
Within Groups	36	26.9	5.6*	0.86	.01 < P < .05

* In favor of the slow readers.

sion, and Table VII, location of information, every classification shows more variation between the good and poor reader groups than within the groups. The classifications where the mean variance within groups is greater than the variance between groups are as follows: Table V, power of comprehension, in general mathematics; Table VI, level of comprehension in grade five, in general mathematics, Latin, and composite achievement; Table VIII, paragraph organization, in general science and Latin; Table IX, speed, in English usage, spelling, general science, algebra, general mathematics, and Latin; Table X, reading speed in grade five, in English usage and general mathematics.

It is also worth while to bring together in one discussion a list of the instances where the differences between the means were in favor of the poor reader group. In Table IV, reading comprehension, and Table VII, location of information, the mean achievement of the good reader group was greater than that of the poor reader group in all classifications. The mean achievement of the poor reader group was greater than that of the good reader group in the following classifications: Table V, power of comprehension, in general mathematics; Table VI, level of comprehension in grade five, in Latin; Table VIII, paragraph organization, in general mathematics and general science; Table IX, speed, in spelling, general science, algebra, general mathematics, and composite achievement; Table X, reading speed in grade five, in general science, algebra, Latin, and composite achievement. However, in all of these instances, except the last two, the ratios were insignificant. In the case of the last two, namely, Latin and composite achievement, the ratios are probably significant.

PICTORIAL PRESENTATION OF RELATIONSHIPS[1]

A drawing in perspective showing the variation in the mean achievement score in ninth grade English associated with joint variation in reading comprehension and IQ is presented in Figure II. The regression equation to predict scholastic achievement in ninth grade English from intelligence and reading comprehension ‘is pictured. The steepness of the slope is the indication of the strength of the relationship between achievement in English and the two background traits. Each IQ segment, three of which are depicted in Figure IIa, shows the regression equation

---

[1] These drawings are included as illustrations, not as a source of argument. They merely depict graphically the slope of relationship. The slope of relationship could have been established by calculating the regression equations in each case.

to predict English achievement from the specific IQ and the various reading comprehension levels. Conversely, each reading segment, three of which are depicted in Figure IIb, shows the regression equation to predict English achievement from the specific reading level and the various IQ levels.

By following each IQ segment it may easily be seen that for every IQ level the better the reading comprehension, the better the achievement in English. Despite the fact that the range in reading comprehension for this group of 300 children is very large, even those who have achieved the most skill in reading comprehension are definitely at an advantage over those whose reading comprehension is but slightly less. Inasmuch as the level of achievement in English increases with ability in reading comprehension in a steady, straight-line fashion, there seems to be no critical level of reading comprehension. In other words, the greater skill one can achieve in reading comprehension the greater will be his chances for successful achievement in ninth grade English. This is clearly shown by looking at the 111 IQ segment. The achievement in English of this group of children with IQ's from 108 to 114 ranges from what would be classified as "F" work to what would be classified as "A" work, and ability in reading comprehension appears to be the determining factor in this range of achievement in English.

The slope in the case of each reading segment below the 96 IQ level is practically level. However, the 81, 88, and 96 IQ segments show increasing mean achievement in English as the higher reading comprehension levels are reached. From this it may be seen that of the group of children at these lower levels of intelligence, those children classified as doing "failing" work will probably be the ones who have the poorest reading comprehension.

In Figure IIb, at reading level 293 an increase in mean achievement in English occurs with increased intelligence. In the case of reading comprehension levels 188 and 398, the mean achievement in English does not show an upward slope, but rather appears fairly level.

These drawings are based upon group means. Predictions from them are valid for groups only and not for individuals.

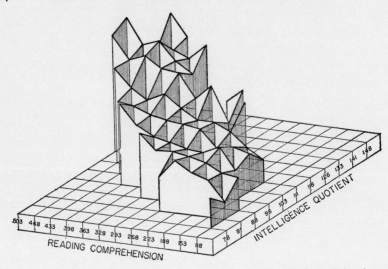

FIGURE II. Mean Achievement Score in Ninth Grade English as Related to Both Intelligence Quotient and Reading Comprehension

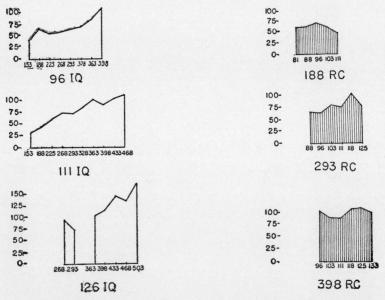

FIGURE IIa. Mean Achievement Score in Ninth Grade English as Related to Reading Comprehension at Each of Three Different Intelligence Quotient Levels

FIGURE IIb. Mean Achievement Score in Ninth Grade English as Related to Intelligence Quotient at Each of Three Different Reading Comprehension Levels

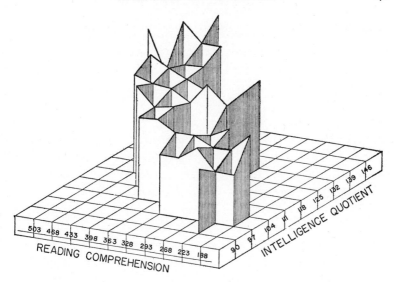

FIGURE III. Mean Achievement Score in Ninth Grade Composite Achievement as Related to Both Intelligence Quotient and Reading Comprehension

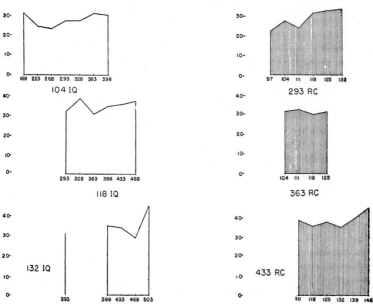

FIGURE IIIa. Mean Achievement Score in Ninth Grade Composite Achievement as Related to Reading Comprehension at Each of Three Different Intelligence Quotient Levels

FIGURE IIIb. Mean Achievement Score in Ninth Grade Composite Achievement as Related to Intelligence Quotient at Each of Three Different Reading Comprehension Levels

READING COMPREHENSION, IQ, COMPOSITE ACHIEVEMENT

A drawing in perspective showing the variation in the mean composite achievement score in the ninth grade college preparatory course associated with joint variation in reading comprehension and IQ is presented in Figure III. Three IQ segments and three reading comprehension segments are pictured in Figures IIIa and IIIb. The mean scores in composite achievement of those groups with high reading comprehension ability and also high intelligence are larger than are the mean scores for those groups of lesser IQ and lesser reading comprehension levels. The three IQ segments (104, 118, and 132), in Figure IIIa, do not show an increase in mean achievement with increasing reading levels, as was evident in Figure II. Reading segment 293, Figure IIIb, shows an increased mean achievement as the intelligence level increases; reading segment 363 is fairly level; and reading comprehension segment 433 is irregular, the highest mean achievement, however, being at the highest IQ level.

Since the composite level of achievement increases with ability in reading comprehension in a steady, straight-line fashion, it does not display a point in ability in reading comprehension above which reading is no longer a factor in composite ninth grade achievement. Just as in the case of achievement in English, the greater the reading comprehension the better are the chances for scholastic achievement in ninth grade school work. This seems to be true regardless of intelligence ratings.

READING SPEED, IQ, SIZE OF VOCABULARY

A drawing in perspective showing the variation in the mean achievement score in English vocabulary knowledge associated with joint variation in reading speed and IQ is presented in Figure IV. Three IQ segments and three speed of reading segments are depicted in Figures IVa and IVb.

The relation between IQ and vocabulary knowledge is shown to be very high. However, a significant relationship exists between speed of reading and vocabulary. This is illustrated by the fact that at each IQ segment an increase in vocabulary occurs as

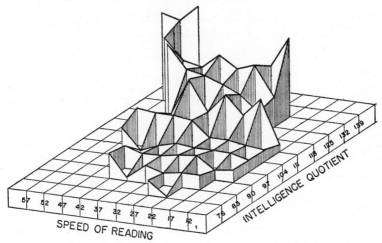

FIGURE IV. Mean Achievement Score in Vocabulary as Related to Both Intelligence Quotient and Speed of Reading

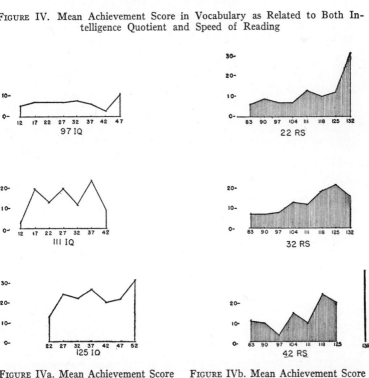

FIGURE IVa. Mean Achievement Score in Vocabulary as Related to Speed of Reading at Each of Three Different Intelligence Quotient Levels

FIGURE IVb. Mean Achievement Score in Vocabulary as Related to Intelligence Quotient at Each of Three Different Speed of Reading Levels

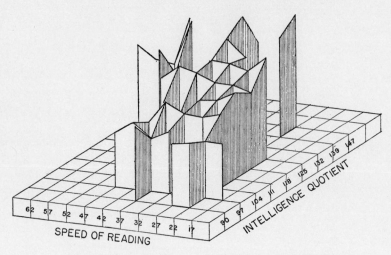

FIGURE V. Mean Achievement Score in Ninth Grade Composite Achievement as Related to Both Intelligence Quotient and Speed of Reading

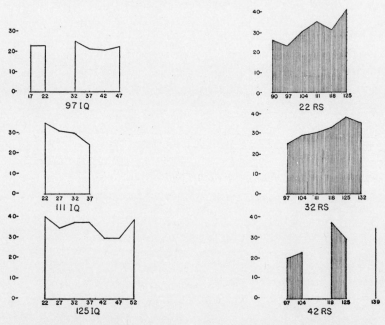

FIGURE Va. Mean Achievement Score in Ninth Grade Composite Achievement as Related to Speed of Reading at Each of Three Different Intelligence Quotient Levels

FIGURE Vb. Mean Achievement Score in Ninth Grade Composite Achievement as Related to Intelligence Quotient at Each of Three Different Speed of Reading Levels speed of reading increases. Speed of reading is highly associated with size of vocabulary. The investigator is not prepared to state, on the basis of this investigation, whether fast reading is a factor in increasing vocabulary or whether a large vocabulary is conducive to fast reading.

READING SPEED, IQ, COMPOSITE ACHIEVEMENT

A drawing in perspective showing the variation in the mean composite college preparatory achievement associated with joint variation in reading speed and IQ is presented in Figure V. Three IQ segments and three speed of reading segments are shown in Figures Va and Vb.

The high relationship between intelligence and composite achievement is illustrated by the drawing itself as well as by the three reading speed segments. The relationship which was established in the earlier statistical work between speed of reading and composite achievement, while not significant, was in favor of the slow readers: that is, the trend was that the slow readers were at an advantage, in general, in composite ninth grade achievement. Figure V as a whole, as well as the three IQ segments, show this same trend in favor of the slow readers. The evidence, while not statistically significant, again points to the fact that the elementary school may be placing too much emphasis upon increasing reading speed and thereby neglecting the problem of increasing ability in other reading skills; as, for example, ability in a work-study technique such as is measured by Test 5 of the Iowa Silent Reading Test.

SUMMARY

By way of summarizing what has already been stated in this chapter, the presentation will be from the point of view of a specific school subject rather than a specific reading measure.

The hypothesis, which is to be tested in each of the relationships studied, is that there is zero difference in the specific scholastic achievement between the two groups (similar in the basic background traits of mental age and chronological age, but different in the specific reading ability under consideration). In order to reject the null hypothesis, the ratio of the mean difference between groups to the mean difference within groups in the specific scholastic achievement must be large enough so that it approaches a magnitude that would not be expected to occur in random sampling of like populations. By comparing the observed value with the value at Fisher's 5 per cent point, 1 per cent point, and .1 per cent point, the significance of the observed value may be ascertained. When the ratio of the greater mean variance to the smaller mean variance is less than the value corresponding to the 5 per cent point, we have failed to reject the null hypothesis. In other words, the data do not reveal a difference. There may be at least three possible explanations: (1) errors of measurement may have increased the variance within groups and consequently decreased the measure of significance of variation between groups; (2) in those cases where the groups are small, a real difference may not have been revealed as significant; or (3) the specific reading ability under consideration may not have been a significant factor in the specific achievement under consideration. Whenever the observed ratio is larger than the value at the 5 per cent point and yet not so large as the value at the 1 per cent point, the observed difference is probably significant. In such a case, by random sampling of like populations a value as large as the observed value would be expected to occur in less than five out of a hundred samples. However, if the observed ratio lies between the 1 per cent point and the .1 per cent point, or if it exceeds the .1 per cent point, the significance is established.

NINTH GRADE ENGLISH

The 1937 Cooperative English Test provides a measure of English usage, spelling, and vocabulary, as well as a measure of achievement in total English. Calculations were made of the analysis of variance of the relationships existing between the various reading skills and each of the three parts of the measurement of achievement in English as well as the total of the three parts. Inasmuch as all the children in the group took a course in ninth grade English, their achievement in English was measured.

The 1937 Cooperative Literary Acquaintance Test was also given to the group.

The highly significant relationships existing between composite reading comprehension and achievement in the five aspects of English, which were studied, show that for successful achievement in ninth grade English children should be taught to read as well as is within their capacity to learn and is feasible. The important conclusion here is that efforts should be made to increase reading comprehension as much as possible, rather than an attempt made to increase it to a specific, critical point.

The highly significant relationship existing between power of reading comprehension and achievement in the five aspects of English again emphasizes the importance of skill in reading comprehension for achieving in grade nine. Children who are able to read comprehensively paragraphs of increasing difficulty have greater potentiality for achievement in English than children who have lesser ability in this aspect of reading.

The highly significant relationships existing between the fifth grade level of comprehension measure and achievement in ninth grade English, in all five of its special aspects, show that the group of children who have a high level of reading comprehension as early as grade five are at a distinct advantage in a ninth grade English class over the group who have not been so fortunate.

Skill in the work-study reading technique is a significant factor in achievement in spelling, but the relationship is not nearly so pronounced as it is in the other four aspects of English achievement. It is indeed remarkable that relationships so highly significant result between achievement in English and the specific skill of using an index when the measure of that skill is based upon only five minutes of testing time.

Skill in paragraph organization[2] has not been shown to be a factor in ability in spelling: that is, skill in outlining does not appear in these data to be of help in the improvement of spelling ability. In the other four aspects of achievement in English, however, skill in this reading ability is definitely a factor.

An analysis of the content of the material contained in the

reading tests in terms of testing time shows that approximately one-third is devoted to social science materials, one-third to materials from the fields of science, five per cent from the field of mathematics; the remaining materials are literary in content. An examination of the English achievement tests and of the literary materials in the reading tests show that, with the exception of the vocabulary items, the materials are rather different. The high relationships existing between the various measures of reading and English achievement, when mental and chronological ages are held constant, justify the statement that achievement in English and achievement in reading abilities are complementary to one another. One can only speculate as to just what factors are contributing to this high relationship, other than actual ability in reading; since both mental age and chronological age are held constant, they are seemingly not factors in the relationship; and apparently only a part of the relationship is accounted for by the similarity of the tests of reading and English achievement.

Speed of reading is a highly significant factor in literary acquaintance and in size of vocabulary. This is also found to be true with regard to reading speed in grade five: that is, those children who were among the fast readers in grade five had the largest vocabularies and the best acquaintance with literature when they were in grade nine. A possible explanation of this fact is that since the rapid readers are capable of reading more material in a given period of time, they would meet and learn a large number of words as well as become comparatively well informed in the field of literature. Explanations in terms of interest might also be offered. For example, other things being equal, the more rapid reader may find greater satisfaction in literature and read more as a consequence; or, the pupils who get the greatest satisfaction from literature may, as a result, spend more time reading and acquire greater speed as a consequence. Only further studies can decide between these and other possible explanations.

---

² In any discussion of relationships based upon these short sub-tests of reading, it is necessary to remember that they are not as valid and reliable as the total test of which they are only a part.

Of the thirty-five relationships discussed in this summary of English achievement, in one only is the difference between the means of the two groups reversed in sign; in the case of spelling the slow readers have greater mean achievement than the more rapid reader group.

In three of the classifications the variance between groups is less than the variance among members of the same group; these are in the case of achievement in spelling and English usage when the groups were separated on reading speed, and achievement in English usage when the groups were separated on the fifth grade measure of reading speed.

NINTH GRADE GENERAL SCIENCE

The 1937 Cooperative General Science Test, Form N, which affords a comprehensive measure of achievement in the various fields of natural science, was given to the 163 children enrolled in general science courses.

The slow reader group in speed of reading, as measured in both grade nine and grade five, appear to have an advantage in achievement in ninth grade general science, although in both cases the relationship is not statistically significant. This trend in favor of the slow readers also appears in scholastic achievement in algebra and in general mathematics. It may well be that the children who are scholastically successful in these less verbal subjects have quite unconsciously developed differential rates of reading and that the speed with which they read scientific material is relatively as fast as the speed with which they read the more verbal material. Or it may be that those children who have learned to read the more verbal material rapidly find it difficult to slow up their rate of reading sufficiently to read, with understanding, material in the fields of science and mathematics. These aspects of reading rate were not studied in this investigation. Had the investigator known in advance just what the findings were to be with regard to the relation between speed of reading and achievement in science and in mathematics, an attempt would have been made to devise tests which would measure rates of reading scientific materials. It is conceivable that the children who are successful in these subjects actually read scientific materials at faster rates than do children whose achievement is less successful. In other words, the children may have developed reading speeds for materials in the fields of mathematics and science which are quite different from the rate they use on other types of reading matter. The fact that the relationship between speed of reading simple materials and achievement in science and mathematics is low suggests a further explanation; namely, that there is little or no relationship between speed in reading simple literary materials for casual understanding, and speed and other skills in reading materials in books on science and mathematics. The latter represent largely specific skills which the slow reader of literary materials may be as likely to acquire as is the rapid reader.

Skill in composite reading comprehension and power of comprehension are highly significant factors in achievement in general science. The children who have achieved ability in these two aspects of reading are at a distinct advantage in mastering the content of their general science course. Ability to use an index is a factor in achievement in general science, but skill in outlining has not been shown to aid such achievement.

The variance within groups is greater than the variance between groups when the groups were separated on skill in paragraph organization and on speed of reading. In other words, the ratios in these two classifications are less than would be expected to occur by chance sampling of like populations.

From the point of view of achievement in general science, the teacher of general science might conceivably find it advantageous to devote a portion of the first few weeks of the course to improving the reading ability of the students in the comprehension of scientific materials.

Ninth Grade Algebra

The achievement of the 107 children who were enrolled in courses in algebra was measured by means of the 1937 Cooperative Elementary Algebra Test, Form N. This test is composed of items covering the application of basic skills and principles of algebra through the subject of quadratic equations. Skill in the use of an index is a highly significant factor in achievement in ninth grade algebra. This work-study technique is more highly related to achievement in algebra than any of the other measures of reading skill included in this investigation. Ability in reading comprehension is a significant factor, but the relationship is not nearly so pronounced as it is in the case of skill in the use of an index.

When the groups were separated on composite speed and on the fifth grade measure of reading speed, the difference between the means is in favor of the slow readers. In the case of composite speed the variance within groups is greater than the variance between groups.

General Mathematics

The achievement of 181 children who were enrolled in courses in general mathematics was measured by means of the 1937 Cooperative Mathematics Test, which includes a wide sampling of mathematical problems.

Skill in the work-study reading ability was the only one of the seven reading skills which showed a significant relationship to achievement in general mathematics. The general mathematics course is perhaps the least verbal of the ninth grade subjects included in this study. The children who were enrolled in the course included all those who did not expect to go on with their schooling upon the completion of high school. The mean IQ as well as the mean reading comprehension ability was lower for this group than for the entire group. The reading abilities used in a subject such as general mathematics were not adequately measured. It is probable that, had a measure of reading comprehension of reading mathematical materials been used, significant relationships would have been the result.

In three of the seven reading classifications (power of comprehension, paragraph organization, and reading speed) the difference between the means is reversed in sign, the poor reader group having greater mean achievement than the good reader group.

In four of the seven classifications (power of comprehension, level of comprehension in grade five, reading speed, and the fifth grade measure of reading speed) the variance within groups is greater than the variance between groups.

Ninth Grade Latin

The achievement of the 88 children who were enrolled in courses in first year Latin was measured by means of the 1937 Co-operative Elementary Latin Test, Form N, which is made up of the reading of Latin passages, the testing of knowledge of Latin vocabulary, and the testing of knowledge of grammatical constructions.

It should be remembered in any consideration of the analysis of variance of Latin achievement that the numbers are relatively small and consequently real differences may not be revealed as significant.

The mean difference in achievement is in favor of the poor reader group in both of the fifth grade reading classifications. In three of the seven classifications (grade five level of comprehension, paragraph organization, and reading speed) the variance between groups is less than the variance among members of the same group.

The relationship which exists between composite reading comprehension and achievement in Latin demonstrates that reading comprehension is definitely a factor in Latin achievement.

The significant relationship in favor of the slow readers in grade five and achievement in ninth grade Latin points to the conclusion that a slow rate of reading of literary materials for some reason goes hand in hand with high ability in mastering the content of a first year Latin course and that a rapid speed of reading goes with low competence in Latin.

COMPOSITE ACHIEVEMENT IN THE COLLEGE PREPARATORY COURSE

One hundred of the 300 children in the group were enrolled in the college preparatory course. Sigma scores of achievement in each of the four major subjects were combined to provide a measure of composite achievement. Many of the previous studies of reading have been based upon some such composite measure of achievement as this. The discussion in this section substantiates the point of view that many subtle relationships are obscured by such a blanket method of procedure.

Reading comprehension is a highly significant factor in composite achievement; yet the relationship between it and one item of composite achievement, namely, general mathematics, is not significant.

Although power of comprehension is a factor in achievement in English and general science and although a highly significant relationship exists between it and composite achievement, the relationships between this reading ability and achievement in the other ninth grade subjects are not significant. A positive relationship between comprehension and composite achievement conceals the fact that power of reading comprehension, at least beyond some minimum lower than most of these children possess, is of very little or no value in the mastery of ninth grade Latin and of general mathematics.

These data are not inconsistent with the hypothesis that level of reading comprehension in grade five is not a factor in composite achievement in grade nine; yet in all five of the aspects of English which were measured highly significant relationships exist.

Skill in outlining is a highly significant factor in four of the five aspects of English; yet in composite achievement, as well as in the five other measures of ninth grade achievement, it has not been demonstrated of value in achievement.

Speed of reading is not reliably related to composite achievement; yet in two parts of composite achievement, namely, literary acquaintance and size of vocabulary, speed is a factor.

A slow speed of reading, as measured in grade five, is positively related to composite ninth grade achievement. This significant relationship conforms to the trend in favor of the slow readers which is apparent throughout a great part of the speed of reading data.

These findings demonstrate the fact that combining achievement into one general measure obscures many of the more subtle relationships which exist between reading skills and scholastic achievement in various school subjects. This detailed study of relationships (seventy in all), showing the relation between various reading skills and various school subjects, suggests:

1. The need for specialization in reading ability to meet the requirements of different subjects.

2. The need for further information about the types of reading skills required in specific subjects at different grade levels, and perhaps, for different total programs, methods of testing, and kinds of activities demanded by tests.

3. The need for teaching reading and study techniques for each subject.

CHAPTER IV

SUMMARY AND CONCLUSIONS

THIS INVESTIGATION was initiated to study in a detailed fashion the relation between various reading skills and scholastic achievement in various ninth grade subjects. The reading skills investigated were:

- A. Reading Comprehension, based upon a composite of reading comprehension on the Traxler, Iowa B, and Shank Silent Reading Tests.
- B. Reading Rate, based upon a composite reading rate on the Traxler and Iowa B Silent Reading Tests.
- C. Power of Comprehension (Traxler, Part III).
- D. Location of Information (Iowa B, Part 5).
- E. Paragraph Organization (Iowa B, Part 3).
- F. A measure of Fifth Grade Level of Comprehension, Modern School Achievement Test, administered May 1933
- G. A measure of Fifth Grade Speed of Reading, Modern School Achievement Test, administered May 1933

Scholastic achievement was investigated in the following areas:

- A. English
  - English Usage
  - Spelling
  - Vocabulary
- B. Literary Acquaintance
- C. Latin
- D. General Mathematics
- E. Algebra
- F. General Science
- G. Composite Achievement in the College Preparatory Course

The degree of relationship existing between each of the reading abilities and each of the scholastic achievement areas was determined by a generalized matched group method whereby the variables upon which the matching was based were mental age and chronological age. Mental age was determined by administering the 1937 Revision of the Stanford-Binet Test of Intelligence, Form L, to the 300 children in the population.

Drawings in perspective were made to show the curve of relationship between specific measures of achievement and IQ and specific reading skills.

The principal findings[1] may be summarized as follows:

1. Varying degrees of relationship exist between the several aspects of ability in reading and composite ninth grade achievement. Ability in composite comprehension, in location of information, and in power of comprehension are all highly significant factors in composite ninth grade achievement. Slow readers are at an advantage in composite achievement. Skill in paragraph organization, as here measured, does not appreciably aid the student in the successful pursuance of ninth grade work.

2. Varying degrees of relationship exist between the several aspects of reading and each of the various ninth grade subjects. The reading abilities essential to achievement in the various subjects differ considerably. The extent to which a reading skill is a factor in achievement depends upon the scholastic achievement in question; the relationship may be highly significant, significant, or not significant, or it may be negatively significant.

3. The importance of ability in the various aspects of reading to achievement in English is quite apparent; the greater the achievement in various reading abilities, the greater will be the achievement in English. While the measures of achievement in English and of achievement in reading comprehension may seem similar, they are rather different because the reading tests include content which is not literary, and because much of the literary materials which is included in the reading tests is different in kind from the materials in the English achievement tests.

4. A measure of reading comprehension in grade five possesses value in predicting scholastic achievement in ninth grade English.

---

[1] In the interpretation of the results it should be remembered at all times that mental age and chronological age were held constant by the statistical method used. It should also be remembered that the measure of skill in paragraph organization and the measure of skill in location of information are based upon scores received on short sub-tests, the validity and reliability of which are not as high as is the case with the longer test of which they are but a part.

It does not appear to be of value in predicting success in the other ninth grade subjects.

5. These data indicate that reading abilities, as measured by the standardized tests, are highly related to achievement in literary areas; and they are not as highly related to achievement in other subject matter areas. They suggest that the children are taught to do the literary type of reading, but that this type of reading does not meet all the needs of the other subject matter areas at the ninth grade level. They further suggest that the development of the types of reading abilities which are useful in mastering the content of ninth grade English is well under way by the end of the fifth grade. The apparent lack of preparation in the reading abilities and techniques needed in the content subjects other than literary of grade nine places a special burden upon the teachers of those subjects. It is customary for the teacher of English in junior and senior high schools to assume responsibility for the teaching of reading. It appears, however, that the teaching of reading skills and abilities specific to subjects other than literary in the junior and senior high school represents the most acute needs and that it should be, in part at least, an integral part of the teaching of those subjects.

6. Skill in work-study techniques is a very real factor in achievement in algebra and in general mathematics. Reading efficiency appears to be a greater factor in achievement than does high ability in various aspects of reading comprehension. If a quite different type of reading test, including the comprehension of formulas and the like, had been used, the results might have been different.

7. The importance of ability in the various aspects of reading comprehension for achievement in ninth grade general science is demonstrated.

8. The study of speed of reading is a very subtle problem indeed. Standardized reading speed tests measure speed of reading relatively easy, non-technical materials. There are no available measures of speed of reading technical literature. One of the conclusions drawn from this investigation is that standardized tests, providing measures of such aspects of reading speed, would con-

tribute to diagnostic and remedial work with high school and college students.

A fast rate of reading simple materials is a definite help in enlarging vocabulary and broadening literary acquaintance; and yet a relatively slow rate of reading of simple material is characteristic of high achievement in science, mathematics, and Latin.

Scientific and mathematical reading requires careful, slow, interpretative reading of comparatively small amounts of material. Ninth grade students are suddenly introduced to quite different subject matter areas, with which they have had little previous experience, and for the mastery of which new reading techniques are required. They attempt to read a mathematical passage at the same rate of speed that they use in reading a novel. Confusion is the inevitable result. Some of the children develop a new speed of reading to use in these different situations. Others experience difficulty in reading required technical material of whatsoever kind and much time and effort is wasted because they are plunged into new, strange fields without having been aided in the acquisition of proper reading speed techniques.

Further investigation is needed to verify or modify the interpretation presented above.

9. The data all indicate that there is no such thing as a critical level of reading ability, above which added skill in reading is no longer a factor in achievement at the ninth grade level, such as Lee[2] found to exist in the intermediate grades (4–6).

In the case of reading comprehension, at every intelligence level increased skill in reading comprehension results in increased achievement in ninth grade English. The curve of relationship is a steady, straight-line one. A steady, straight-line curve of relationship is likewise found between skill in reading comprehension and composite ninth grade achievement.

These data are not in accord with other data[3] in that they do not point to a grade score of 7.0 as a minimum essential for successful achievement in junior-high-school work. They indicate

[2] Lee, Dorris May, *The Importance of Reading for Achieving in Grades Four, Five, and Six*, 1933, p. 60.
[3] *Thirty-Sixth Yearbook*, p. 75.

rather that any increase in reading ability will be reflected by increased scholastic achievement.

10. The importance of diagnostic and remedial work in reading on the junior and senior high school levels is demonstrated.

11. "Every teacher should be a teacher of reading." The importance of this trend, stated by The Committee on Reading in the *Thirty-Sixth Yearbook of the National Society for the Study of Education,* is well illustrated by this study as is also the need for carefully planned guidance in reading throughout the ninth grade.

SUGGESTED PROBLEMS FOR FUTURE STUDY

1. It would be interesting to extend this study to the senior high school and college levels.

2. Studies of the various reading skills required in each subject, as well as in the various phases of each subject, in the high school and college curricula could profitably be made.

3. It would then be worth while to ascertain whether and to what extent it was profitable to teach those various reading abilities before beginning the teaching of various subjects, or a phase of a specific subject.

4. The study of reading speed begun here should be extended. Is reading speed a general attribute or does the same person have varying relative rates of speed for varying types of materials?

5. A study should be made of the reading requirements of achievement tests. Would the results have been different if quite different types of achievement tests had been used, such as essay writing, discussions, speeded versus non-speeded tests, outlining or various other types of answers?

6. A study should be made of the same relationships in quite different types of schools. For example, would the same relationships appear among pupils taught by less formal methods or in programs in which more extended and diversified reading, with less dependence on single texts, is employed?

BIBLIOGRAPHY

ANDERSON, E. M. *Individual Differences in the Reading Ability of College Students.* University of Missouri Bulletin, Vol. XXIX, No. 39, 1928.

BOND, ELDEN A. "A Method of Selecting Sub-normal Children for a Vocational School." *Journal of Juvenile Research,* Vol. XXI, July, 1937, p. 188.

BROOKER, IVAN ALBERT. *The Measurement and Improvement of Silent Reading Among College Freshmen.* University of Chicago Libraries. 1934.

BUSWELL, GUY THOMAS. *How Adults Read.* Supplementary Educational Monographs, No. 45. University of Chicago, 1937.

CENTER, STELLA S. AND PERSONS, GLADYS L. *Teaching High-School Students to Read.* D. Appleton-Century Co., 1937.

Cooperative Achievement Tests. A Handbook Describing Their Purpose, Content, and Interpretation. The Cooperative Test Service of the American Council on Education, 1936.

Educational Records Bulletin, No. 21. "The Public School Demonstration Project in Educational Guidance." Educational Records Bureau, 1937.

Educational Records Bulletin, No. 20. "The 1937 Achievement Testing Program of the Educational Records Bureau." 1937.

EURICH, ALVIN G. *The Reading Abilities of College Students: An Experimental Study.* College Problems Series. University of Minnesota Press, 1931.

FISHER, R. A. *Statistical Methods for Research Workers.* Oliver and Boyd, London, Sixth Edition, 1936.

GARRETT, HENRY E. *Statistics in Psychology and Education.* Longmans, Green and Co., 1926.

✓ GATES, ARTHUR I. *The Improvement of Reading.* The Macmillan Company, Revised Edition, 1935.

GEBERICH, J. R. "Five Years of Experience with a Remedial Reading Course for College Students." *Journal of Experimental Education,* Vol. 3, 1934, pp. 36–41.

GRAY, W. S. "Reading Difficulties in College." *Journal of Higher Education,* Vol. VII, October, 1936, pp. 356–62.

GREENE, H. A., JORGENSEN, A. N., KELLEY, V. H. *Iowa Silent Reading Tests Manual of Directions.* World Book Company, 1931.

HATHAWAY, GLADYS. "Purposes for Which People Read: A Technique for Their Discovery." *University of Pittsburgh School of Education Journal,* Vol. 4, 1929, pp. 83–89.

HORN E. AND MCBROOM, MAUDE. *A Survey of a Course of Study in Reading.* Extension Bulletin No. 93, College of Education Series No. 3. University of Iowa, 1924.

JOHNSON, PALMER O. AND NEYMAN, J. "Tests of Certain Linear Hypotheses and Their Application to Some Educational Problems," *Statistical Research Memoirs,* Vol. I, June 1936.

JORGENSEN, A. N. "Use of Diagnostic Tests in Teaching Silent Reading," *Elementary English Review*, Vol. 9, April, 1932, p. 86.

LEE, DORRIS MAY. *The Importance of Reading for Achieving in Grades Four, Five, and Six.* Contributions to Education, No. 556. Bureau of Publications, Teachers College, Columbia University, 1933.

McCALLISTER, JAMES M. "Reading Difficulties in Studying Content Subjects." *Elementary School Journal*, Vol. 31, pp. 191–201.

McCALLISTER, JAMES M. *Remedial and Corrective Instruction in Reading.* D. Appleton-Century Company, 1936.

McKEE, PAUL. *Reading and Literature in the Elementary School.* Houghton Mifflin Company, 1934.

SCRIBNER QUIZ. "How Well Do You Read," *Scribner's Magazine*, January, 1938, pp. 88–89.

SHANK, SPENCER. *Student Responses in the Measurement of Reading Comprehension.* C. A. Gregory Co., 1929.

STRANG, RUTH. *Behavior and Background of Students in College and Secondary School.* Harper & Brothers, 1937.

STRANG, RUTH. *Improvement of Reading in Secondary Schools.* Bureau of Publications, Teachers College, Columbia University, 1935.

Teaching of Reading: A Second Report. Thirty-Sixth Yearbook of the National Society for the Study of Education, Part I. Public School Publishing Company, 1937.

TERMAN, LEWIS M. AND MERRILL, MAUD A. *Measuring Intelligence.* Houghton Mifflin Company, 1937.

THORNDIKE, E. L. "Improving the Ability to Read." *Teachers College Record*, Vol. 36, October, November, December, 1934.

THORNDIKE, E. L. "Reading Is Reasoning: A Study of Mistakes in Paragraph Reading." *Journal of Educational Psychology*, Vol. VIII, June, 1917.

THORNDIKE, E. L. *A Teacher's Word Book of the Twenty Thousand Words Found Most Frequently and Widely in General Reading for Children and Young People.* Bureau of Publications, Teachers College, Columbia University, 1931.

TIPPETT, L. H. C. *The Methods of Statistics.* Williams and Norgate, Ltd., Second Edition, Revised, London, 1937.

TRAXLER, ARTHUR E. *Teacher's Handbook for Traxler Silent Reading Test.* Public School Publishing Company, 1934.

WITTY, PAUL A. "Diagnosis and Remedial Treatment of Reading Difficulties in the Secondary School." *Educational Trends*, Vol. 3, April, 1934.

WITTY, PAUL A. AND LA BRANDT, LOU L. "Some Results of Remedial Instruction in Reading." *Educational Trends*, Vol. 2, January, 1933.

VITA

Eva Bond, born July 15, 1903, at Chehalis, Washington.

Academic Training: B.S. degree, Teachers College, Columbia University, 1926. M.S. in Commerce and Industry, University of Alabama, 1932.